Welcome to our program centered on Recovery from White Conditioning. As you embark on a lifelong journey of self-exploration and growth, we invite you to hold on to whatever has led you to these pages: curiosity, hope, pain, or frustration. We hope you will use those forces to propel you forward on your recovery journey.

Table of Contents

Introduction

In a 2014 interview, Ta-Nehisi Coates, a senior editor at *The Atlantic*, explained: "We talk about race a lot, we do. You know, I think it's wrong to say we don't talk about it...we do. I don't think we talk about it in depth as much as we should. Part of the problem is that, when you start talking about it in depth...when you say everything we are, everything we have, is built on past sins—that the things are tied...when we start recognizing that there's something congenital: It's as if I had a problem with alcohol. And I could say, 'OK, but I'm just gonna go into the bar and not have a drink. I'm gonna be OK. I don't need to have any sort of a conversation.' That's a different conversation in that *I have to confess to the fact that I'm an alcoholic...that there's something in me...that that's here...that I will always have to cope with that...that I will always have to deal with that.* The honesty that that takes, the courage that takes, the strength that takes is pretty profound."

It is our hope that the 12 step journey ahead of you will inspire you: to summon profound honesty, courage, and strength; to apply those qualities in pursuit of a deeper understanding of yourself and others; and to invest in a lifelong journey of recovery from white conditioning.

As Paolo Freire asserted: "No one can be authentically human when he prevents others from being so." It has also been said that "no one is free when others are oppressed." Join us as we examine the ways in which white supremacist ideology lives in us and around us, whether we've invited it in willfully or not. Join us as we move actively toward our own freedom and fullest version of our humanity by fighting against and recovering from white supremacist teachings.

TECHNICAL NOTES: In this Recovery Program, we are clear to use terms like "white supremacy," "white supremacist conditioning," and "the ideology of white supremacy." Founders of our program were clear: by embracing these terms (instead of "racism" or "racist conditioning"), we work to avoid a common deflective practice in which white people accuse people of color of being "racist" toward them. While we could proceed to explain that racism is defined as "race prejudice PLUS power," we prefer, instead, to call out the ideology of white supremacy as the specific type of racism that exists, systemically, in the United States of America. Furthermore, if we can embrace the painful, ugly reality of white supremacy as an organizing ideology that affects every aspect of life in our society, we can work hard to name and claim this dark truth that lives in us and around us...so that we may then pursue a recovery journey toward love and light with ourselves and our fellow human beings.

If you find yourself struggling to hear, accept, or understand definitions or proposed recovery efforts within these pages, we invite you to A) know that you're not alone and B) visit our website for a wide variety of resources and tools to guide you on your recovery journey. The text that follows is intentionally designed to *not* focus on proving that the ideology of white supremacy exists in us and around us. Countless community members, activists, historians, culture critics, and thought leaders have spent their lives developing perspectives and tools that are necessary and helpful in our recovery journey. We encourage all recovery group participants to seek out those sources of wisdom on an ongoing basis, growing intimately familiar with their perspectives and turning to them when distressed. We also encourage you to trust that your lived experiences and recovery efforts can offer wisdom back to your recovery group peers, as none of us can do this work in isolation.

We need each other to call us forward in our recovery, as we strive and struggle to reclaim our full humanity. We hope this text offers you a guiding framework for that lifelong journey.

12 Steps of Recovery from White Conditioning

1.) We admitted that we had been socially conditioned by the ideology of white supremacy…that our minds were subject to racial biases, often unconsciously so.

2.) We came to believe that we could embrace our ignorance as an invitation to learn.

3.) We developed support systems to keep us engaged in this work.

4.) We journeyed boldly inward, exploring and acknowledging ways in which white supremacist teachings have been integrated into our minds and spirits.

5.) We confessed our mistakes and failings to ourselves and others.

6.) We were entirely ready to deconstruct previous ways of *knowing*, as they had been developed through the lens of white supremacy.

7.) We humbly explored new ways of understanding...proactively seeking out new learning and reconstructing a more inclusive sense of reality.

8.) We committed ourselves to ongoing study of our racial biases, conscious or unconscious, and our maladaptive patterns of white supremacist thinking.

9.) We developed strategies to counteract our racial biases.

10.) We embraced the responsibility of focusing on our impact, more than our intentions, in interactions with people of color.

11.) We engaged in daily practices of self-reflection.

12.) We committed ourselves to sharing this message with our white brothers and sisters...in order to build a supportive recovery community and to encourage personal accountability within our culture.

STEP 1: We admitted that we had been socially conditioned in accordance with the ideology of white supremacy—that our minds were subject to racial biases, often unconsciously so.

The first step to any kind of recovery is admitting that we have a problem. Individuals not ready to acknowledge a problem may be unable to pursue and receive the help they need. Becoming aware of a problem – and admitting it to others – can be challenging, but it is a fundamental step on the recovery journey.

Before we proceed a moment further, we must first acknowledge our context. The School of the Americas Watch defines "White Supremacy" as "an historically based, institutionally perpetuated system of exploitation and oppression of continents, nations, and peoples of color by white peoples and nations of the European continent, for the purpose of maintaining and defending a system of wealth, power, and privilege." The definition continues to describe white supremacy as "a system, a web of interlocking, reinforcing institutions: economic, military, legal, educational, religious, and cultural. As a system, white supremacy affects every aspect of life in a country."

In the United States, the ideology of white supremacy has been consistently utilized to enact, defend, and perpetuate centuries of oppression against people of color, including the Indigenous people of this land and enslaved individuals of African descent. While terms like "system of exploitation" and "system of oppression" may tempt us to consider that we, as individuals, are not intimately connected to or responsible for the suffering of people of color, it is important—and, ultimately, liberating—to acknowledge that we, as white people, do, inescapably, have a relationship with and, in countless ways, benefit from oppressive, white supremacist systems.

We know that hearing and embracing the term "white supremacy" is often a painful experience. We are all aware of emboldened, self-identified "white supremacists" who actively participate in vitriolic actions of bigotry and hate, such as members of the Ku Klux Klan and Neo-Nazi groups. Let us assure you that, in acknowledging our connection to the ideology of white supremacy, we are, by no means, declaring that we belong to the same category as bona fide hate group members. We are, however, calling out beliefs in the superiority of the white race as a pathological condition, which affects some of us, as white people, far more severely than others. We are also declaring that none of us, as white people living in a society organized by white supremacy, escape our social conditioning unscathed.

For recovery group purposes, it is often helpful to think of white supremacist conditioning affecting us, as white people, on a spectrum. Individuals at one extreme are living out white supremacist ideals through hateful actions and overt racism, while individuals at the other end of the spectrum actively invest, every day, in fighting back against their white supremacist conditioning. If you consider yourself as existing somewhere in between these two extremes, or are not yet ready to place yourself on the spectrum, know that you are sharing a space with individuals who are striving to engage in honest self-reflection, working to determine their placement today alongside their hopes for tomorrow.

As we work to evaluate the degree to which white supremacist conditioning has affected who we are today, it is worthwhile to first consider the various sources of our learning about race — ours and others' — that have shaped us to date.

From the moment of our birth, we are inundated with new learning. Our minds constantly develop new neural pathways through sensory input (what we see, hear, touch, taste, smell, intuit) from the world around us. When we pause to think about all of the things we've learned in our lives — and all of the ways in which we've acquired that learning — we can reflect on how remarkable we are as biopsychosocial organisms, traversing the earth.

Our learning happens through explicit, intentional actions (i.e. parents verbalizing the rules for crossing the street), and it happens through more implicit means (i.e. noticing that our white mother clutches her purse when she sees a black man walking toward her). As children, learning can happen in the presence of caring adults who help us organize new information. Learning can also happen in the complete absence of caring others…or in the presence of individuals who are confused, hurt, angry, and afraid.

Studies routinely show that small children, as young as two years old, have already developed a strong sense of racial preference. In the United States, young children of all races disproportionately indicate that pale-skinned children are "good" and dark-skinned children are "bad." Where does this learning come from? In what ways were you, yourself, exposed to ideas that uplifted the humanity of your fellow white men and women, while denying the humanity — or not even acknowledging the existence — of other races? If you, as a child, expressed curiosity about people with different skin colors, how did grown-ups react to you? Did they encourage you to grow in understanding about racial differences while affirming our common humanity? Or did they anxiously "shhhh" you to avoid the "taboo" subject of race altogether?

However we have arrived at this moment, through learning that occurred via family conversations, academic institutions, history books, news media, and countless other pathways, we now come together, in solidarity, to confront and begin recovering from past learning tied up in white supremacist ideology. By stepping outside of our individuality and examining the context in which we find ourselves—white people living in a society organized by white supremacy—we are called to name and claim the context of our lives. As we step out of denial, out of a white supremacist world in which we don't fully see or value our brothers and sisters of color, an entirely new, multicultural universe opens up to us.

Unfortunately, for individuals who are either still living in denial or fully invested in living out white supremacist ideals, we often see that there's an overwhelmingly strong desire to hold on to past learning. Like all recovery programs, this program only works if the individuals involved are committed to and invested in working their steps. Individuals may only benefit from recovery processes if they are willing to examine their inner selves and their external context, rejecting the myth of white supremacy in all its forms.

In management circles, it is often said that "10% of your employees will take up 90% of your time." The saying is designed to highlight that, while managers may spend the vast majority of their times problem-solving the challenges brought forth by a small minority of their employees, the remaining 90% of their hard-working employees, often, go unnoticed and unappreciated. For the purpose of our recovery groups, it is important for us to focus on the metaphorical "90%" of individuals who are willing to embrace the 12 steps of recovery. While we may continue to reach out to the "10%" and "call them in" to grow in new understandings, we commit ourselves, first and foremost, to prioritizing support of individuals who express a willingness to pursue recovery — or at least to consider trying.

Our greatest goal is to "call in" the most people to do this work: to recognize that their humanity is at stake and that they can invest, actively, daily, in recovering from white supremacist conditioning. Even if the "10%" are turned off by our efforts, we can take comfort, at minimum, in knowing that we are shifting the paradigm. We are ceasing to perpetuate ideas that involve white people: pitying people of color; feeling plagued by white guilt to the point of inaction; or perceiving ourselves as heroic in the fight for racial justice.

We are, instead, declaring what we deeply believe to be true: we must work, every day, to save ourselves…to fight against the ugliness and hate in our world, tied up in white supremacist teachings that live in us and around us…so that our children can envision and work to create a more kind and just world, in which humans of all racial backgrounds are seen, valued, and allowed to live free.

STEP 2: We came to believe that we could embrace our ignorance as an invitation to learn.

We acknowledge that we, as white people, will never know what it feels like to walk in the world as a person of color. We embrace our "not knowing" as a powerful reminder of our ongoing need for new learning, and we abandon white supremacist traditions of "knowing" how others should feel, think, and act.

For so long, we, as white people living in a white supremacist society, have been encouraged to believe that our way — of being, seeing, understanding — is the *right* way. As we have been conditioned to see the world around us in ways that maintain our worldview, we have grown quite comfortable.

It has felt comforting to believe that the world is "basically a good place," that discriminatory practices of our nation's history are relics of the past, and that anyone who works hard can make it in America. The myth of meritocracy (which assures us that we all get to our positions in society simply by nature of our hard work and ability) is regularly shared as American gospel. While these ideas tempt us with their feel-good, simplistic assertions that our society is living out ideals of fairness and equality, it is essential to our recovery that we recognize these beliefs as inherently false.

The myth of meritocracy, alongside the widely circulated myth of a "post-racist society," hurts our cause. Moreover, holding tight to these beliefs limits our ability to grow and to expand our thinking. In recovery, we find that there is greater power, within ourselves and in community with others, to embrace a stance of not-knowing as an active step in countering white supremacist patterns. Ignorance, therefore, is the essential starting place for our work.

Embracing ignorance offers us the opportunity to start: from a place that acknowledges our limitations; from a place that frees us from the illusion that we could fully understand the pain of others (in this case, people of color in a white supremacist society); and from a place that allows us to embrace a lifelong journey of learning, based on our recognition that the finish line of a thriving, respectful, multicultural society lives well beyond our immediate reach.

Ignorance also serves as a spiritual foundation of our work. What freedom might we experience in no longer clinging to our own understandings? What profound meaning might we gain by letting go of beliefs limited by our conditioning...of beliefs created in isolation from groups of humans who experience our society in significantly different ways? What new world might we imagine and help co-create if we accept a starting point that involves us, as white people, acknowledging our incessant need for new learning and human connection to guide our path?

In our day-to-day interactions, it is common to hear white people asserting statements like: "I just don't understand why Black people protest on highways" or "I don't understand why undocumented immigrants break the rules in coming to this country." Such statements are most often made in a spirit of condescension and judgment.

With condescension in one's perspective, there is no opportunity for new learning. If, however, a person were to make the statement with an aim and tone reflective of one who is pursuing new understandings, there is much potential for new growth: "I don't understand why Black people protest on the highways...I have no lived experience that informs me of a pain or fear so great as to disrupt 'business as usual' and risk my freedom in the process. I wonder what that pain or fear or frustration might be, and I wonder how I might find those answers."

The above example demonstrates that we are not abandoning the topics that we don't know; we are, instead, tending to those matters with an awareness of our ignorance and an invitation to connect, humanely, with new learning and growth. Our ignorance is real and undeniable. Our courage to own it and chart new paths from its presence encourages us on to Step 3.

STEP 3: We developed support systems to keep us engaged in this work.

We are aware that facing and recovering from the effects of white supremacist conditioning will involve difficult, sometimes painful, moments. We commit to developing practices that facilitate self-care...to ensure that we are gentle with ourselves while also bravely able to confront the dehumanizing ideology of white supremacy.

"Be gentle with yourself. You are a child of the universe, no less than the trees or the stars. In the noisy confusion of life, keep peace in your soul."
–Max Ehrmann

How do we, as children of the universe, "keep peace in our soul" amid the pain and injustice swirling around us? How do we strive to be loving and gentle toward ourselves while also committed to attacking white supremacist ideology — as it lives in us and around us — with consistency and courage?

There are no easy answers to these questions, though we implore all persons striving for recovery to live with and respond to these questions daily. As we declare throughout the recovery process, "person in context" language affords us a reminder of our unique personhood: our passions, quirks, memories, dreams, strivings, and failings. "Person in context" language also reminds us of our specific context: we are white people living in a society organized around the ideology of white supremacy. It is this precise context that necessitates our ongoing recovery efforts, in addition to actions, pursuing justice and transformation, which emerge outside of our recovery group spaces.

Within our recovery journey, within ourselves, our groups, and our broader community, we insist upon a commitment to self-love and self-care. Spirituality and faith may play a role in self-care practices, though we encourage all individuals to pursue their own definitions and plans for how they will care for themselves while doing this work. If faith is a source of comfort for us, we may strive to implement consistent rituals that will anchor us in our recovery journey, such as daily prayer, weekly attendance at places of worship, or regular reading of spiritual texts. We may pray new prayers, including requests of our Higher Power to "give us courage in facing painful realities of our life here on Earth…realities we'd prefer no longer existed…but realities that must be faced if they are to be eradicated." We may ask our Higher Power for guidance and support in keeping our hearts and minds open to new learning.

For those of us who do not embrace a Higher Power that is known by others, we may still embrace a spirit of faith that can give us courage amid darkness. That faith may be rooted in the recovery group process: believing that individuals coming together to intentionally grow is, in and of itself, worth the effort. Or we might live out a belief in the spirit of innovation: of trying new strategies to solve complex problems, knowing that we have no guarantee of resolution, but appreciation for the journey.

For many of us, our other identities may seemingly impact our ability to invest in self-care. If we are financially poor, for example, we may believe we cannot afford to offer ourselves additional acts of kindness. If we are mothers, we may firmly believe that others' well-being takes precedent above our own. For the sake of our recovery, we *must* find ways to take care of ourselves, if only by practicing radical self-love: being gentle in our thoughts and understandings of ourselves as humans who are striving. We may hum or sing or stretch or sigh to provide some relief to our bodies and brains that are, too often, overwhelmed with stress and pressure. We may identify relationships in our lives that offer us a sense of safety and unconditional love: relationships with individuals who are going to reassure us that we are loved, in spite of our mistakes, and who will encourage us to keep growing. We may also embrace a mantra of "I'll try again tomorrow" or "I'll never give up" as part of honoring our commitment to recovering our full humanity.

The overarching point is that we *must* invest in doing what we can to remain engaged in this work, honoring self-care as an investment in our recovery.

Steps 1-3, Important Reminder:

It is common for individuals in recovery to spend significant time working the first three steps. While it may be tempting to speed through them to expedite the overall process, being authentic with ourselves is essential to solidifying our foundation for recovery. If we move too quickly, before we've completed the first three steps with sincerity and commitment, we risk jeopardizing our long-term recovery goals. Specifically, we risk moving into an ever-growing awareness of the complex, lifelong recovery journey ahead of us, without a simultaneously growing confidence in ourselves, our ability to persevere through new pain, and the strength of our support systems and practices. For many who have not devoted much energy to the first three steps, they have grown weary from the tasks required for recovery and have, as a result, suspended or regressed on their journey. Others have rushed through the first few steps, believing that they will be able to remain invested in an intellectual exercise of "recovering" without ensuring safe spaces and places to land on the bumpy journey.

While we encourage all individuals pursuing recovery to spend as much time as they authentically need to in order to establish a solid foundation through the application of steps 1-3, it should also be noted that we can, simultaneously, remain open to learning and applying steps beyond the first three.

STEP 4: We journeyed boldly inward, exploring and acknowledging ways in which white supremacist teachings have been integrated into our minds and spirits.

After acknowledging the problem, we must also acknowledge that it has impacted many areas of our lives, consciously and unconsciously. Each of us must explore ways, past and present, in which the ideology of white supremacy has negatively impacted us: our understanding of history, our social networks, and our patterns of interacting with people of color, with an emphasized focus on microaggressions.

It has been said that we spend countless hours running from knowledge of ourselves. As white people, in particular, we direct a lot of energy toward avoiding difficulty: difficult introspection, difficult topics of conversation, and potential confrontation with others. We may establish rules about "no religion or politics" at the dinner table, or we may quickly try to change the subject when someone tells a racist joke at a holiday gathering. In work circles, we may remain silent when a supervisor makes a racist comment and wrestle with ourselves, internally, not knowing what to say in response.

Before we can determine how to respond to overt racism that appears in the world around us, we must first venture deep inside of ourselves to unearth the ways that we, too, have internalized messages of white supremacy. Any such internal exploration requires fortitude of spirit, as well as tools for uncovering portions of ourselves that are often hidden. In recovery, we believe that internal exploration is enhanced through community with others, as the journey toward inner truth can be overwhelming and too intimidating to be made alone.

Pursuing honest reflections of ourselves requires tremendous courage. This type of self-study is essential to progress in our recovery and encompasses various facets of ourselves and our understandings. Three areas have been identified above: our understanding of history, our social networks, and our patterns of interacting with people of color, though there are countless other areas in which we may grow in knowledge of ourselves to further inform our recovery efforts. Tools designed to enhance the self-study process referenced above can be found at the recovery website, while we may also engage in honest exploration and assessment of ourselves in our recovery groups and in self-designed ways.

STEP 5: We confessed our mistakes and failings to ourselves and others.

Beyond identifying ways in which our thinking, feeling, and relating have been impacted by white supremacist conditioning, honestly addressing the actions that have emerged from that conditioning is a separate, necessary step. Confessing past (and ongoing) microaggressions to a group and receiving support is an essential part of recovery.

It has been said that our human instinct is to run away from our shame...to avoid facing the hurt we may cause others or to deny that we made a mistake. It has also been said, however, that, if we step in to our shame, fully embracing and accepting it, we can be liberated from it.

A young recovery group member recounts a moment in which she was describing her compassion for "illegal immigrants." A white middle-aged man immediately stopped her and asserted: "You know better than that. No human being is illegal." She recalls being shocked and ashamed in that moment. She had never intended to use language that was hurtful...yet, despite her best intentions, she had, indeed, perpetuated language that dehumanized a group of people and their circumstance. In that moment, she felt she had two options: 1) tuck her tail between her legs and run away, shrinking and disappearing in to oblivion or 2) swallow her momentary shame and embrace new learning, new vocabulary, that would help her continue to live out her compassion toward undocumented workers.

Today, she uses this example with others who are nervous about making mistakes on the journey. She names the experience of using hurtful language and of being corrected in a way that felt extremely direct; takes ownership of her previously "not thinking about" how easily we repeat language and terms that don't originate from a place of common humanity; and shares her mistake — and her growing beyond the mistake — as an example of the way we can liberate ourselves from thinking we've got it all figured out and, instead, embrace humility with grace.

While we may debate over effective strategies for "calling out" actions rooted in white supremacist ideology or "calling in" people to the cause, when we, ourselves, are confronted with an awareness that we have made a mistake on our journey, we are presented with an important opportunity: to run from our mistake or to stay and face it.

"Mistake," it should be noted, is a widely-used term that, in our recovery efforts, can be lifted up as an indication that more learning is required. If we sit with our self-identified mistakes, as well as our actions called out by others as hurtful or unhelpful, we can think of those moments as opportunities to acknowledge our failing to live out our recovery ideals. We can then be supported by fellow humans who are also striving — and, at times, failing — in facing the painful and important awareness that this recovery journey is lifelong.

Rejecting white supremacist ideology, which is often tied up with perfectionist tendencies, means that we free ourselves to try to move differently in the world, humbly accepting the limitations of our humanness, and loving ourselves and others through our mistakes. Confucius reminds us: "Our greatest glory lies not in never falling, but in rising each time we fall."

May we always recognize failing as part of learning. May we rise to the challenge of holding space for humans who are striving to become better and wiser than they were yesterday. And may we always nurture and challenge each other beyond our mistakes.

STEP 6: We were entirely ready to deconstruct previous ways of *knowing*, as they had been developed through the lens of white supremacy.

After admitting these problems (white supremacist conditioning and related actions), it is then time to let go of "knowledge" developed in isolation from people of color.

For many, step 6 is a painful step in their recovery journey. As white people living in a white supremacist society, we have grown accustomed to *knowing* things and having our "knowledge" embraced as truth.

Acing history exams has made us feel confident in our understanding of our nation's past, yet we failed to acknowledge that such learning was (most often) based on "*his*tory" written from European American perspectives. We have rarely undertaken a pursuit of knowledge about global history and contemporary realities from diverse perspectives. And we have lived amid rampant cultural appropriation, which often leads us to believe that white people invented everything under the sun. Step 6 is centered on the often uncomfortable process of moving from "knowing" to not knowing. Taking that step requires us to tolerate ambiguity and uncertainty, which some may not be brave enough to do.

Individuals in recovery are encouraged to engage in perpetual self-and communal-examination. As it relates to the teaching of U.S. history, important questions must be poised: why, for example, do we call white people in this country's history "settlers" and "pioneers" instead of "conquerors" and "perpetrators of genocide"? Can we collectively acknowledge that, if history were written from the perspective of enslaved Africans in the South or Indigenous peoples whose lands were stolen, our understanding and telling of U.S. History would be vastly different and profoundly painful? If we can acknowledge that the perspectives of people of color are left out of mainstream his-storytelling, can we agree that it is time to reject mainstream history and knowledge as the primary source of information?

In regards to this step, it is also important to note that our "knowledge" about history extends to the present moment. We continue to tell ourselves stories about who we are, who "the others" are, and how we must act in relation to each other. Preparing ourselves to let go of all of the things we've been told about the "heroes" and "evildoers," today and throughout history, is an essential step that takes us back to our earliest days of childhood, in which we *knew* so clearly that there were "good guys" and "bad guys" in the world. We did not, however, know that such classification was frequently tied up in racialized reflections and understandings of the world around us.

If we can wrestle, within ourselves, beyond the painful awareness that everything we've been taught has been largely tinted through the lens of white supremacist ideology, we can prepare ourselves for a rebirth of sorts…a letting go of information and processes that have proven unhelpful in furthering our own humanity. Doing so requires that we feel prepared to stand strong in the recovery work that we've accomplished—and vow to continually invest in—in steps 1-5, while undertaking step 6.

STEP 7: We humbly explored new ways of understanding...proactively seeking out new learning and reconstructing a more inclusive sense of reality.

This step involves mindfully and intentionally engaging in learning to more deeply understand the experience of people of color in a white supremacist society. This type of learning can take place in a variety of ways, including: reading texts written by people of color, actively listening to the experiences of people of color, patronizing businesses owned by people of color, etc.

By the time we've arrived at Step 7, we are well aware that white-centered, comfortable ways of learning have limited our ability to understand: to know ourselves more deeply and to understand the experiences and feelings of our brothers and sisters of color. We need radically different tools, sources of information, and learning experiences in order to develop a worldview that expands our thinking, seeing, feeling, and believing.

Active listening can be a completely new and effective strategy, if undertaken with a seriousness about listening to others' pain. More often than not, we do not listen to understand; we listen to respond. When communicating across racial difference, if we, as white people, are in a defensive space, not prepared to actively listen and tune in to the perspective being shared with us, we will fall back in to perpetuating white supremacist patterns. We will also miss out on new learning and new perspectives that could assist us toward our recovery goals. Active listening—listening empathically to the experience of another human, paying full attention to understanding their truth—is a skill that requires significant effort and practice, especially as another's truth may threaten our preferred, comfortable beliefs.

Beyond active listening, which is a practice that is good for all people in all circumstances, there are efforts that we, as white people, can apply to advance our progress toward recovery. These efforts are rooted not only in increased learning about general lived experiences and wisdoms of other cultural communities; they should also reflect a commitment to understanding the survival strategies that communities of color have embraced amid ongoing assaults on their humanity, enacted by white supremacist ideology.

In general, there is an endless amount of new learning that we can welcome in to our lives to grow a more comprehensive, inclusive understanding of the world around us. As it has been said, "Other cultures are not failed attempts at being you. They are unique manifestations of the human spirit." If we, as white people, open ourselves to learning about these unique manifestations, our lives are sure to improve as we benefit from multiple perspectives.

At the same time, we must honor and respect the survival strategies undertaken by individuals and communities enduring brutalization and dehumanization by systems designed to annihilate them. Without an understanding of the ways that white supremacy — and other forms of oppression — have hurt groups of people, we cannot fully appreciate the strength and brilliance of groups who have persevered through the pain. By pursuing a deeper understanding of the wisdom, creativity and resourcefulness that have sustained communities for centuries, alongside the courage and pain involved in surviving oppressive structures, we seek to develop a profound respect for our brothers and sisters of color that is vital for our recovery.

To pursue such understanding, we commit ourselves to changing habits. We intentionally seek out information on: businesses owned by people of color, texts written by thought-leaders of color, art showcases featuring artists of color, etc. We may also strive to build relationships with people of color, while ensuring that we are never doing so in order to reach a certain "quota" of friends of color that would help us feel more accomplished in our recovery. We also know that many communities in our nation are relatively homogeneous as related to matters of race. When building such relationships is not an authentic or even viable option, we hold tight to a belief that we can embrace the tasks listed above as part of building new awareness.

We know that these perspectives and experiences will not naturally fall in to our lap without some level of intentional seeking, which we must initiate. White supremacy lives on through the dominating perpetuation of stories told from white perspectives, wealth concentrated in white hands, advertisements positioning white as ideal, and countless other messages that uplift the value of whiteness in our society. We work Step 7 continually to fight those patterns and honor multiple perspectives.

STEP 8: We committed ourselves to ongoing study of our racial biases, conscious or unconscious, and our maladaptive patterns of white supremacist thinking.

This step is about identifying our triggers to negative thoughts (or other stereotypes, positive or negative) about people of color. We remain curious about the source of our thoughts, fears, and assumptions…and perpetually aware of their existence.

In combating any disease or condition that causes human pain and suffering, it is essential to acknowledge the existence of the condition *and* to study its presence in — and impact on — one's life. For individuals living with diabetes, it is important to pay attention to caloric intake and to notice when glucose levels become too low, requiring other types of intervention. In the case of someone struggling with depression, it is not enough to know that depressive symptoms exist; one must also pay attention to circumstances that exacerbate those symptoms. For example, if depressive symptoms increase when a young man visits his verbally abusive uncle, it would behoove the young man to, first, become aware of that challenging circumstance and its impact on his functioning…and, second, to explore and implement strategies that help to reduce the levels of hurt in his life related to his uncle. Whatever he decides: staying away from him, asking friends to attend family events alongside him, inviting his uncle in to a family therapy session…his decision-making process is entirely his own. Step 8 is not about resolving the challenge but, rather, asserting that a resolution cannot be made if we do not, first, notice and understand causal factors or patterns related to our suffering.

As a white person living in a white supremacist society, studying our thoughts, fears, and assumptions about people of color requires us to, again, reject the idea of a "post-racist" society and, instead, confront our own, internal maladaptive patterns of white supremacist thinking. In the case of a white woman who clutches her purse when a young black man walks by, it is important for her to notice that reaction, examine its intensity, and question the source of her fears.

Too often, we label others who don't fit in to our white-centered world as "maladaptive," assuming that they, somehow, have failed to assimilate in to mainstream culture. We fail, however, to consider the inappropriateness of our expectations that a person or an entire community might contort themselves to meet standards rooted in white supremacist ideology. We fail to honor that anyone who is behaving in ways that professionals might deem "maladaptive" while living in systems not designed for their survival might, in fact, be behaving in the most appropriate, righteously rageful ways as systems of oppression continue to hurt them and their loved ones.

In our recovery, instead of allowing our thoughts to be continually dominated by ways in which "others" have failed to be like us, we can courageously look at our own demands of adherence to our world view as a flawed, "maladaptive" expectation. Additionally, like the examples listed above of diabetes and depression, we can commit ourselves to noticing the times in which we feel afraid of, annoyed by, or judgmental toward people of color. It is also important to note that racial biases can affect our thinking in ways that are subtle and not, at first glance, negative in nature. For example, for Asian Americans, the "model minority" stereotype often means that white people regard people of Asian descent as quiet, well-behaved, and intelligent. While this stereotype might not seem as hurtful as more violently offensive stereotypes made against other communities of color, it is essential to note that all stereotypes, generalizing an entire people with complete disregard for their individuality, cause hurt to our common humanity. For Asian American students struggling academically, not only might they struggle to accomplish their coursework, they may also feel doubly challenged as they are "failing" to live up to widespread notions of who they are. For white people on a journey of recovery from white supremacist conditioning, it is important to question all preconceived notions and racial biases about cultural communities, whether they seem positive or negative in nature.

From the awareness of our racial biases, we may engage in further study regarding the propaganda, common narratives, and other vehicles which have been used, today and throughout history, to instill those biases in us. Once we have begun a process of self-studying our biases, we are then ready to continue that exploration, while also acting differently, as directed in Step 9.

STEP 9: We developed strategies to counteract our racial biases.

Developing positive associations to counter negative thoughts is an important, proactive strategy in recovery from white supremacy. We believe that the most powerful way to develop positive associations is to develop authentic relationships with people of color. In lieu of such relationships, we can still engage in daily, proactive practices to retrain our brain from the ill-effects of white supremacist conditioning.

Once we have come, face to face, with the thoughts, feelings, and behaviors tied up in our white supremacist conditioning, and once we have committed ourselves to ongoing self-study, it is then time to imagine and create a worldview in which we expand our ways of being, specifically related to how we understand and connect with people of color. Relationships with people of color — or with anyone who is deemed "different" from us — are routinely lifted up as the best way to reduce biases we possess. Building authentic relationships with people of color, without explicitly pursuing a "quota" of friends from each cultural community, is an important task on the road to creating a thriving, multicultural society.

It must be said, however, that relationships are not enough, in and of themselves. In the best case scenarios, in which relationships across racial difference are rooted in true respect and deep love, it is still essential for white people to continue working their steps, as our conditioning does not instantly —

or ever — entirely fade away from our being. In less ideal scenarios, in which white people *have to* work or associate with a person of color but have not yet committed themselves to their recovery journey, the "relationships" that exist may prove completely ineffective at reducing the racial bias present in white people. If relationships with people of color are simply tolerated, white people will experience little, if any, growth. And more commonly, if relationships with people of color maintain the status quo — or, more specifically, involve white people refusing to acknowledge the role and presence of whiteness in their relationship and in the world — no true transformation will take place.

Outside of developing authentic, loving relationships with people of color, we have hope in our recovery as we consider innovative strategies that we can apply anytime, anywhere. One recovery group member shares her common practice of driving down a city street, saying aloud, quietly to herself, to the men and women of color on the sidewalks: "Hello my brother. Hello my sister." Another recovery group member cites filling up her social media newsfeed with artists and activists of color so that she may be inspired and challenged by their perspectives throughout her day.

Like an individual struggling with depression and ongoing negative self-talk, the idea of implementing positive self-talk — of countering negativity with a kinder, gentler alternate perspective — is an essential part of managing the disease. Similarly, in recovery from white conditioning, white people are encouraged to consider any and all strategies that invite positive associations related to people of color in to their cognitive awareness. While prioritizing positive associations does not mean that other cultural communities possess only positive traits, it is important to reinforce that we, as white people, have been inundated with negative messages about those who are "different" from us. By amplifying the positive, truthful elements of other racial groups, confidence in our ability to hold more complete understandings of our fellow human beings grows.

STEP 10: We embraced the responsibility of focusing on our impact, more than our intentions, in interactions with people of color.

Taking responsibility for the impact of our actions is an ongoing part of recovery. If we fall back into perpetuating white supremacist ideology – or defending actions that have caused hurt to people of color – it's important to stop and admit it. Prioritizing impact, instead of explaining the intent of our behavior (i.e. "I didn't mean to offend you"), is essential for attending to the human being in front of us.

Once we've been working our steps, especially steps 7 and 9, we experience an excitement about an ever-expanding worldview that incorporates and honors multiple perspectives. We may be connecting with people we'd never encountered before; we may be learning traditions and wisdoms from other cultures that enhance our own lives and interactions with our family members; and we may begin sharing some of our learning with individuals in our immediate circles.

If we already have personal relationships with people of color, we may be feeling increasingly connected to their lived experiences, encompassing both joy and suffering. If we've only begun building relationships with individuals who identify as people of color, we may be feeling both the excitement of new human connection as well as the fear of stumbling in our efforts to connect across difference.

In all cases, it is important to remember: we will stumble. Let's say that again: we will stumble.

No one ever said that connecting across difference would be easy. How could it be? Imagine that all men and women grew up on separate islands, reading about each other only in books. Imagine that some, though few, encountered each other occasionally when exchanging goods at a midpoint in the ocean, between the islands. If all men and women were then ordered to move to a shared island, after never encountering or understanding each other personally, how many ways could we envision actions or statements being wildly misinterpreted? How many ways might we hurt or offend each other based on preconceived notions of "the other" gender? In this overly simplistic analogy, we can come to embrace that connecting with groups of people we've rarely, if ever, connected with prompts us to prepare for some missteps.

In the case of white people interacting with people of color in a white supremacist society, we are bound to say and do things that are hurtful to people of color, whether intentionally or unintentionally. Tending to the impact of our actions must become and remain an ongoing priority.

Unfortunately, many white people prefer to focus, instead, on their intentions, defensively asserting that they "didn't mean to" hurt a person of color by what they said or did. As Dr. Ken Hardy asserts, intentions are "the province of the privileged; impact is the province of the subjugated." White people can elaborate, endlessly, about ways in which people of color have misunderstood the intention of their statements, while people of color, meanwhile, are living with the ongoing impact and hurt of microinvalidations and other forms of aggression/microaggressions. While intentions do matter, to some degree, we would never recommend explaining one's intentions, first and foremost, if they drove over someone's toe. Imagine a driver stepping out of their vehicle to assert that "it was not my intention to drive over your toe" as opposed to shouting: "Are you OK? I'm so sorry. Should we call 911?" How selfish and self-centered it would be to focus primarily and exclusively on how one "didn't mean to" cause any hurt.

As in previous steps, the importance of humility for white people cannot be overstated. We must embrace that we will stumble, bump our heads, and certainly not be perfect on this journey toward recovering our full humanity. The more we, again, consider that perfectionism is a by-product of white supremacy (which we are striving to reject), the more we can accept our status as mere mortals…and proceed with compassion for individuals and groups whom we hurt along the way, caring more about their pain than about our self-image or status as being "well-intentioned."

It must be repeated over and over: we are fighting for our own humanity. While we often observe and appreciate the tangible benefits of connecting across cultural differences, we must resist the common white supremacist tactic of commodifying such cross-cultural phenomena. We must hold tight to the belief, beyond striving to build a multicultural society that honors and benefits from various perspectives, the most immediate goal of our recovery is the saving of our own soul. In the name of achieving such a goal, we must remain forever humble, owning up to our failings and fumblings, acknowledging that our conditioning has led us to build up defenses that, ultimately, separate us from our fellow humans. Investing in our recovery means that we can regain a sense of deep-rooted compassion for human beings and strive to, never again, prioritize our comfort over taking responsibility for pain we cause in others.

STEP 11: We engaged in daily practices of self-reflection.

Reflecting on the day — on moments in which we confronted our own white supremacist conditioning and on moments in which we were still bound by its limiting beliefs — is an investment in our recovery. Relevant spiritual practices may play a helpful role in this step, as a way to encourage us toward continued growth and connection, beyond our mistakes.

On our recovery journey, we must always remember: we are keeping score for ourselves, no one else. In addition to the self-study we embraced in step 4, it is also wise to ensure that we have sources of love and support to continually nurture our recovery process, even if those sources exist only in our reflective capacity as humans.

In a space of self-reflection, we can commit to becoming better than who we were yesterday…to becoming more fully human and free from the constraints of white supremacist conditioning. For individuals who embrace spiritual practices as part of their self-care work in Step 3, it makes tremendous sense to apply those practices, again in Step 11, at the end of the day. Self-reflecting alongside faith that one is loved, in spite of any failings that took place, can be a profoundly effective way to continue taking stock of a day's worth of growing. Without official religious or spiritual practices, the act of self-reflecting, in and of itself, can serve as our connection to a world and journey that is much bigger than us, alone. Knowing that other white people are striving, struggling, succeeding, failing, and trying again offers us comfort on our recovery journey.

How does self-reflection compel you to keep moving forward in your life? How do you embrace this practice with grace and kindness toward yourself, while also utilizing reflective capacity to challenge yourself to keep growing tomorrow? How do you hold space for forgiveness of self and new possibilities for connection with others in the days ahead?

STEP 12: We committed ourselves to sharing this message with our white brothers and sisters…in order to build a supportive recovery community and to encourage personal accountability within our culture, every day.

Assisting others to seek help in recovering from white supremacist conditioning and in becoming an ally with people of color is a core component of recovery. Working with future recovery-from-white -conditioning groups is a common choice for this step.

In our recovery program, we lead with love. We recognize that we are all growing in understanding white supremacy — and our relationship with it — from different starting places. On our journey of recovery, we know that the consciousness-raising required for progress will evoke painful, important new levels of awareness. By committing ourselves to share our message with our white brothers and sisters: in ways that nurture and challenge, in ways that involve participation in formal recovery groups and in other, less formal interactions…we embrace a spirit of accountability for ourselves and our people.

This demand for accountability is essential to progress in our recovery journeys. It is common for white people (who are not in recovery) to speak inaccurately on what they see as failed community responses to complex problems. A ubiquitous example of this inaccurate condescension is seen in the common white response to incidents of police brutality or police murder of unarmed black men (and other people of color). Many white people defensively and reflexively cry out: "What about black-on-black crime?" While we will not delve in to the statistics that indicate that the vast majority of all crime is intra-racial (including white-on-white crime), nor elaborate on the countless ways in which community groups and churches in the black community have been working to reduce violence for decades, what we *will* call out as our primary responsibility is to ask ourselves, continually, questions like: What are *we*, as white people, doing to end *our* legacy of violence? What are we doing to actively resist white supremacy as it lives in us and around us? What are we doing to show up for racial justice, working as allies with — and following the lead of — people of color?

It is our explicit hope that this model's focus on internal exploration and growth would, immediately or progressively, translate to anti-racist actions outside of ourselves and the walls of our groups. To be clear, as you've well-learned, the core components of this model do not involve 12 "action steps" that are part of a nation-wide, organized protest, boycott or other broad strategy for dismantling white supremacy. (It is certainly hoped that communities of white individuals, connecting with themselves and each other through the recovery process, would more consistently reach out to people of color in aligned efforts to dismantle broad, systemic injustice. While we do not have the answers of what that precisely looks like, we do believe we can: move differently in the world, understand our relationship to white supremacist structures and practices, and resist them in increasingly innovative ways, if we're willing to start with ourselves.)

We ask you to love yourself, relentlessly, amid the important, challenging journey of recovery. We ask you to lovingly welcome in more white people to the opportunities for healing and growth that exist for all of us, if we're willing to work our recovery program. We encourage you to do so with humility, accountability, and grace, knowing that our humanity is on the line: may we fight, alone and together, each day, to recover and reclaim it.

For additional resources, please visit our website at: www.recoveryfromwhiteconditioning.com